Memories of Mary
The RMS Queen Mary in Pictures Volume I: Construction of 534

by

Thomas Cornwall

Copyright 2017-

Also by the same author:

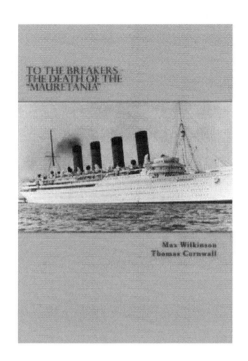

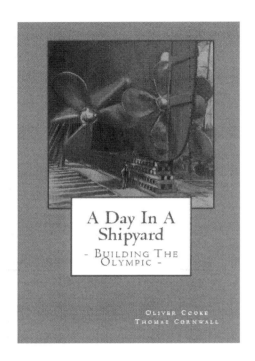

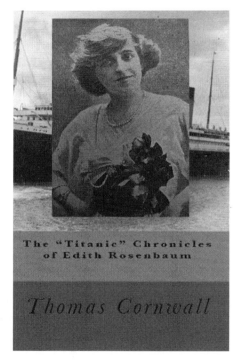

Introduction

Welcome to the first in a proposed three or four (depending on demand!) volume photographic record of the early years of the Cunard-White Star Liner RMS Queen Mary, from model tests, to her keel been laid and finally, to her triumphant arrival in New York following the completion of her maiden voyage.

There have been many, many fine books which detail the minutiae of the Queen Mary's career and I felt that this book should be a celebration of her life in pictures. To this end, the captions are kept to a minimum; indeed many come from the original sources. The ship was not named until very close to launching, and thus I have referred to the hull as "534."

The photographs have come from a variety of sources; postcards, original images, newspapers and journals. Consequently the quality varies from grainy to near pin-sharp. It is hoped that the variation does not interfere with your pleasure!

There is one other point to remember; I have tried, where possible, to maintain a chronological order to the images but sometimes, in an effort to group similar photos together (the stern frame, propellers etc.) I have had to occasionally break this rule. My apologies if this causes some consternation.

I hope you enjoy this wallow in nostalgia.

Thomas Cornwall

The RMS Queen Mary in Pictures
Volume I:
Construction of 534

by
Thomas Cornwall

An 18 foot long self propelled scale model of 534 being tested in John Brown and Co's Clydebank shipyard. A new device produces waves regulated to gale force while the model dashes at speed up and down. Here she is fighting a 60 knot gale.

(Top) the keel soon after being laid and (bottom) the inner bottom partially framed, looking forward.

Work continues as the Canadian Pacific Liner "Empress of Britain" of 42,000 tons is being fitted out.

The bow takes shape as work on the shell plating continues.

Views of the internal structures and decks.

Work on the starboard upper superstructure decks reaches its conclusion.

Looking aft, this excellent view shows the area of the bridge and forward superstructure being plated.

This view and the next picture show two photographs of the forecastle taken within a short space of time, demonstrating the rapid progress being made and the installation of new elements, such as capstans.

In the top photograph, while work on 534 continues, good progress is also being made with the Canadian Pacific liner "Minnedosa" of 15,186 gross tons.

In late 1931, the global financial situation deteriorates so much that work on the hull is suspended until new funding can be secured. Thankfully, the British Government steps in with much-needed money.

Work on the plating of the stern progresses...

…..and is concluded.

The stern frame of 534 is completed at the Darlington Forge company.

Eight castings of the stern frame and shaft brackets, the biggest ever made at that point, being transported from the Darlington Forge to John Brown and Co via the LNER.

The mould used for the propellers

....and the finished version, made by the Manganese Bronze and Brass Co.Ltd. of London

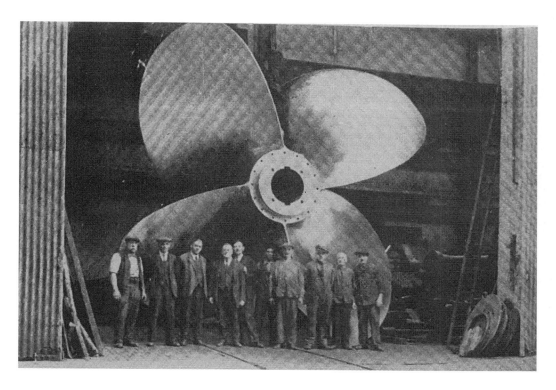

The first of four propellers arrive, delivered at London Docks from Deptford for shipment to the Clyde. It weights over 33 tons, is made of manganese bronze known as "Turbiston" and is 19 feet 6 inches in diameter. Its cost is about £7000.

The third of four propellers is loaded on board the SS "Longships" at Surrey Commercial Docks.

The third propeller is delivered

Finally, the stern of the 534 is finished, leaving the leviathan ready for launching.

The ship on the stocks as seen from Garnieland, Inchinnan

A majestic view: two proud workers admire the fruits of their handiwork.

Printed in Great Britain
by Amazon

13979331R00027